D1758288

9112000393517

SKELETON

WRITTEN BY JOHN WOOD
AND HARRIET BRUNDLE

BookLife
PUBLISHING

©2019
Book Life
King's Lynn
Norfolk PE30 4LS

ISBN: 978-1-78637-460-8

Written by:
John Wood &
Harriet Brundle

Edited by:
Kirsty Holmes

Designed by:
Amy Li

All facts, statistics, web addresses and URLs in this book were verified as valid and accurate at time of writing. No responsibility for any changes to external websites or references can be accepted by either the author or publisher.

PHOTO CREDITS

Images are courtesy of Shutterstock.com. With thanks to Getty Images, Thinkstock Photo and iStockphoto.

Front Cover – svtdesign, Jane Kelly, GoodStudio, Humannet, PixMarket, y wissanustock, R2D2, revers, J.R.Picture, Stefano Garau, cornflower. Master Images – Incomible, Andrew Rybalko (Seymour), Olesia Misty (vector bones), Lemberg Vector studio (header texture), Humannet, R2D2 (background images), Flas100 (paper scrap vectors), 2 – MriMan, 4 – Big Pants, Serega K Photo and Video, J.R.Picture, Blend Images, 5 – 3DStock, rumruay, 6 – eAlisa, Dan Kosmayer, Olga Bolbot, ConstantinosZ, 7 – Andrey Tegin, Alila Medical Media, 8 – cornflower, wavebreakmedia, Kawitsara, 9 – DenisNata, Marcin Balcerzak, 10 – Choochin, Potapox Alexander, Croisy, Alex Mit, wavebreakmedia, 11 – fizkes, Matvienko Vladimir, Life science, 12 – Andrey Tegin, Teeradej, NosorogUA, 13 – Jodie Adams, Robert Kneschke, 14 – eAlisa, 3DMI, ABO PHOTOGRAPHY, 15 – Alex Mit, Kasa1982, 16 – Ekaterina Markelova, 17 – sciencepics, eranicle, 18 – Martin Dallaire, Potapov Alexander, Martynova Anna, Pretty Vectors, 19 – Monkey Business Images, margouillat photo, 20 –martin81, J.R.Picture, Xray Computer, Methavee Eklund, 21 – Rudchanko Liliia, New Africa, 22 – Puwadol Jaturawuttichai, Crevis, 23 – gritsalak, Jan H. Andersen, 24 – Sudowoodo, Stefano Garau, marina_ua, ,25 – 5 second Studio, NONGNUCHZ, 26 – Ninell, Rvector, Morphart Creation, 27 – struna, maxcreatnz, 28 – MriMan, Eric Jennings, Puwadol Jaturawuttichai, Skalapendra, 29 – Juan Aunion, Rocketclips, Inc, oksana2010, 30 – paintings, Thorsten Schmitt.

CONTENTS

Words that look like **this** can be found in the glossary on page 31.

THE MOST
AMAZING
MACHINE

There is a machine that can solve difficult problems. It can learn complicated things. This machine can move around and jump up high. If the machine gets a **virus**, it can often cure itself – and if the machine gets broken, it can often fix itself. It is made up of **billions** and billions of parts, and it even grows bigger.

THIS MACHINE... IS THE HUMAN BODY.

YOUR BRILLIANT BODY

Every day, your body does incredible things to keep you alive. You are probably not even aware of what it is doing most of the time. However, under your skin, all the parts of your body are working together to keep you healthy and ready for the day ahead. Do you ever think about what happens to your food after it disappears down your throat? Or why your body becomes so snotty, sweaty and sick-y when you are ill? What about how you can breathe without thinking? Your body does a lot of things **automatically**.

YOUR BODY IS ALWAYS LOOKING OUT FOR YOU AND HELPING YOU OUT.

EVERY BODY NEEDS A BRAIN

Your brain, sitting in your head right now, is the most amazing part. Human brains are so complicated that we still don't really understand everything about them. There are around 100 billion nerve **cells** in the brain – these are the things that carry messages around the brain and body. But, the brain would be pretty useless on its own. What makes the body amazing is how it all fits together. It's time to go under your skin and find out how it all works.

THE HUMAN BRAIN

THE DOCTOR IS HERE

Hi! My name is Seymour Skinless, and I am the world's smallest doctor – the only doctor small enough to go under the skin and find out exactly what's wrong! You there – you must be my assistant. Well, you are just in time – we have a patient here who is very ill. I think there is something wrong with his skeleton. You know what a skeleton is, right? Well, don't worry, soon you will know all about them – we are about to go inside his body and find out all about it.

Right, let's shrink you down to my size and go inside...

WHAT IS A SKELETON?

The skeleton is a collection of hard bones that are joined together. The bones create the frame for everything else in your body. Think about when you hang up your coat. Without the hanger, your coat would fall in a pile on the floor. It's the same with the human body and the skeleton.

DIFFERENT KINDS OF BONES

Apart from making you human-shaped, your skeleton has many other jobs too. It protects important body parts, it helps you move around and it creates blood cells. Bones come in many shapes and sizes, depending on their job. Flat bones protect our body, long bones are for movement, and short bones are there to help us carry our weight. Some bones aren't like any others – these are called irregular (say: ih-reg-you-la) bones. These include the bones that make up your face.

THE SKELETON KEEPS HUMANS SHAPED LIKE HUMANS.

WHEN MOST PEOPLE THINK OF BONES, THEY THINK OF LONG BONES LIKE THESE. BUT THERE ARE MANY OTHER TYPES IN OUR BODIES.

BONES MAKE UP 15% OF YOUR BODY WEIGHT

WHAT ARE BONES?

A baby has around 300 bones, while an adult has 206. This is because some bones **fuse** together as people get older.

You might think a bone is lifeless, but did you know your bones are actually alive? They are always hard at work, changing and growing, just like lots of other parts of the body. Bones have different layers, each of which has an important job.

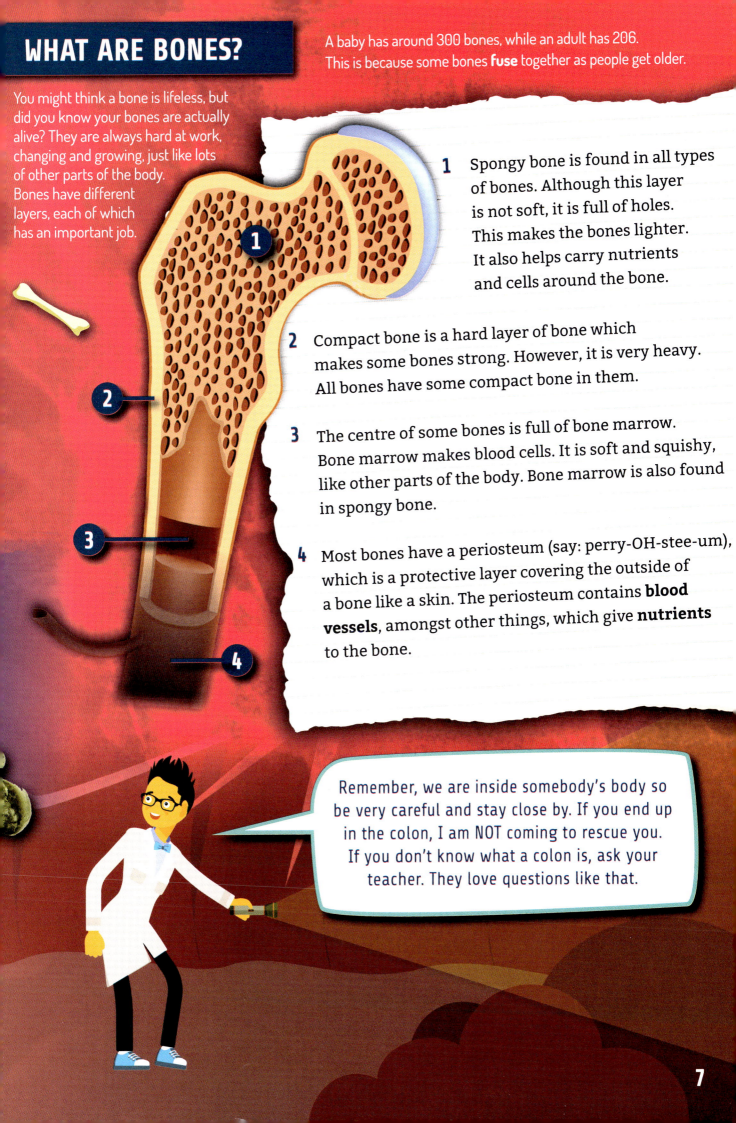

1 Spongy bone is found in all types of bones. Although this layer is not soft, it is full of holes. This makes the bones lighter. It also helps carry nutrients and cells around the bone.

2 Compact bone is a hard layer of bone which makes some bones strong. However, it is very heavy. All bones have some compact bone in them.

3 The centre of some bones is full of bone marrow. Bone marrow makes blood cells. It is soft and squishy, like other parts of the body. Bone marrow is also found in spongy bone.

4 Most bones have a periosteum (say: perry-OH-stee-um), which is a protective layer covering the outside of a bone like a skin. The periosteum contains **blood vessels**, amongst other things, which give **nutrients** to the bone.

Remember, we are inside somebody's body so be very careful and stay close by. If you end up in the colon, I am NOT coming to rescue you. If you don't know what a colon is, ask your teacher. They love questions like that.

FIRST STOP:
FEET

Why start at the feet, I hear you ask? Well, there are 26 bones in each foot – put together that is about a quarter of the bones in your whole body. THAT's why we're starting at the feet!

KNOW YOUR JOINTS

The feet (and hands) are very complicated, and have a lot of bones inside them. This is because they need to move in a lot of different directions. To do this, they have a lot of different joints. Joints are where two bones meet. There are lots of different kinds of joints. Some joints, like those in your back or those in your skull (called sutures) don't move much, or don't move at all. However, most joints, especially in your **limbs**, move a lot. For example, hinge joints open and close, like a door. Your elbows and knees are hinge joints. Ball and socket joints can move in any direction. Your hips are ball and socket joints, which is why you can move your legs in any direction.

A GLIDING JOINT IS WHERE FLAT BONES ARE HELD TOGETHER, BUT THEY CAN GLIDE OVER EACH OTHER EASILY. YOUR ANKLE IS A GLIDING JOINT, AND IT LETS YOU MOVE YOUR FOOT IN ALL DIRECTIONS.

Pivot joints allow parts of the body to **rotate** or twist. There is a pivot joint in your neck which lets you look left and right. The ellipsoid joint sounds complicated, but it isn't. It lets you move something back and forth and side to side. These are the joints between the bottom of your fingers and your hands. Try it – hold up your hand and move your first finger while keeping it straight. It can go towards you, away from you, or side to side.

THIS IS YOUR INDEX FINGER.

SYNOVIAL FLUID

Most joints in the body that we use for movement are called synovial joints. This is because they are covered in a special **fluid**, called synovial fluid. The fluid is important for two reasons. Firstly, it stops the bones rubbing against each other, which would damage them. This is the same reason why we put oil on bicycles – the bicycle runs much more smoothly when there is fluid between the different parts. Secondly, the synovial fluid also gives nutrients to the parts of the bones that it covers.

NUTRIENTS KEEP THE BONE HEALTHY AND ALIVE.

Cartilage is another **tissue** inside your body that stops bones rubbing together at the joint.

LOOK — LEGS!

Your legs are much simpler than your feet. There are only eight bones in the legs, but they are some of the longest and strongest in your body. The bones in your legs have to be strong because they carry all of your weight while running, walking and jumping.

THE FEMUR (THE BONE IN YOUR THIGH) IS THE BIGGEST BONE IN YOUR BODY.

KNEE JOINT

TENDON

HOW DO BONES MOVE?

Bones in the body are moved by muscles and tendons. Muscles are made of tissue. They are able to contract, which means they get smaller. This is what happens when you squeeze your muscles. When the muscles contract, they pull on tendons, which are strong lines of tissue that attach muscle to bones. For example, when you squeeze certain muscles in your leg, the muscles get smaller and pull on the tendons, which pull on the bones in your big toe. This makes your big toe move! If your skeleton was a puppet, the tendons would be the strings and the muscles would be the hands controlling the strings.

Look! If I move these tendons, I can make him pick his nose!

This is very undignified, Seymour!

MANY MUSCLES

Squeezing muscles only pulls tendons in one direction. However, most of your joints move in many directions. So how do we do that? Well, there are often lots of muscles that control the same joint. For example, there are two main muscles that help you bend your knee. Your hamstring muscle is at the back of your thigh. When your hamstring contracts, the tendons pull the bone up, which bends your knee. To make your knee straight again, the hamstring relaxes, and another muscle, called your quadricep muscle, contracts. The quadricep is at the front of your thigh. The quadricep tendons pull the bones so your knee and leg become straight again.

HAMSTRING

QUADRICEPS

Of course, you don't have to think about what muscles you need to squeeze when moving. You can even move lots of different muscles at the same time – you can walk, talk and hold things with your hands all at the same time! This is what makes the human body and brain so amazing.

ALL OF THESE THINGS HAPPEN IN AN INSTANT.

STRAIGHT UP THE
SPINE

WHAT IS YOUR SPINE?

Your spine is your backbone. But your spine isn't one long bone – it is made up of lots of little ring-like bones all joined together. Each little bone is called a vertebra. You might be able to feel them – they feel like little bumps going down the middle of your back and neck.

THERE ARE 26 VERTEBRAE IN MOST PEOPLE.

THE SPINE ISN'T COMPLETELY STRAIGHT — IT IS NATURALLY A LITTLE BIT CURVED.

THE SPINAL CORD

One of the important jobs of the spine is to protect the spinal cord. The spinal cord is a bundle of nerves that run through the hole in each vertebra. Nerves are cells which send **signals** between your brain and your body. If you want to move your hand, a signal is sent from your brain to the muscles in your hand. The signals are carried by nerve cells. If something happened to your spinal cord, you might not be able to send signals to some parts of your body, such as your legs. Luckily, the spinal cord is well-protected by the vertebrae in your spine.

THE VERTEBRAE GET THICKER AND LARGER AS THEY GO DOWN. THIS IS BECAUSE THE ONES NEARER THE BOTTOM HAVE MORE WEIGHT TO CARRY.

SPINAL DISCS

Between most of your vertebrae, there are spinal discs. Spinal discs have **gel**-like insides and cartilage on the outside. They are like small cushions between your vertebrae, and they are there to **absorb** shocks when you jump up and down or run.

IF THE DISCS WEREN'T THERE, YOUR VERTEBRAE WOULD HIT AGAINST EACH OTHER AND BE DAMAGED.

People are around one centimetre shorter by the end of the day. This is because the discs in the spine get thinner when **pressure** is put on them. However, they get thicker again when sleeping, so people are taller again in the morning.

TWIST AND SHOUT

THE TOP TWO VERTEBRAE, CALLED THE ATLAS AND AXIS, GIVE YOU THE MOST MOVEMENT IN THE SPINE.

There are joints between all the vertebrae which let you bend and twist your back. The top seven vertebrae are called the cervical spine. The cervical spine connects your backbones to your head. They let you move and twist your neck.

Well, there's nothing wrong with this part of the patient. This is a fine spine. We better keep going – we've got to get to the ribcage before it's too late!

GO RIGHT AT THE
RIBCAGE

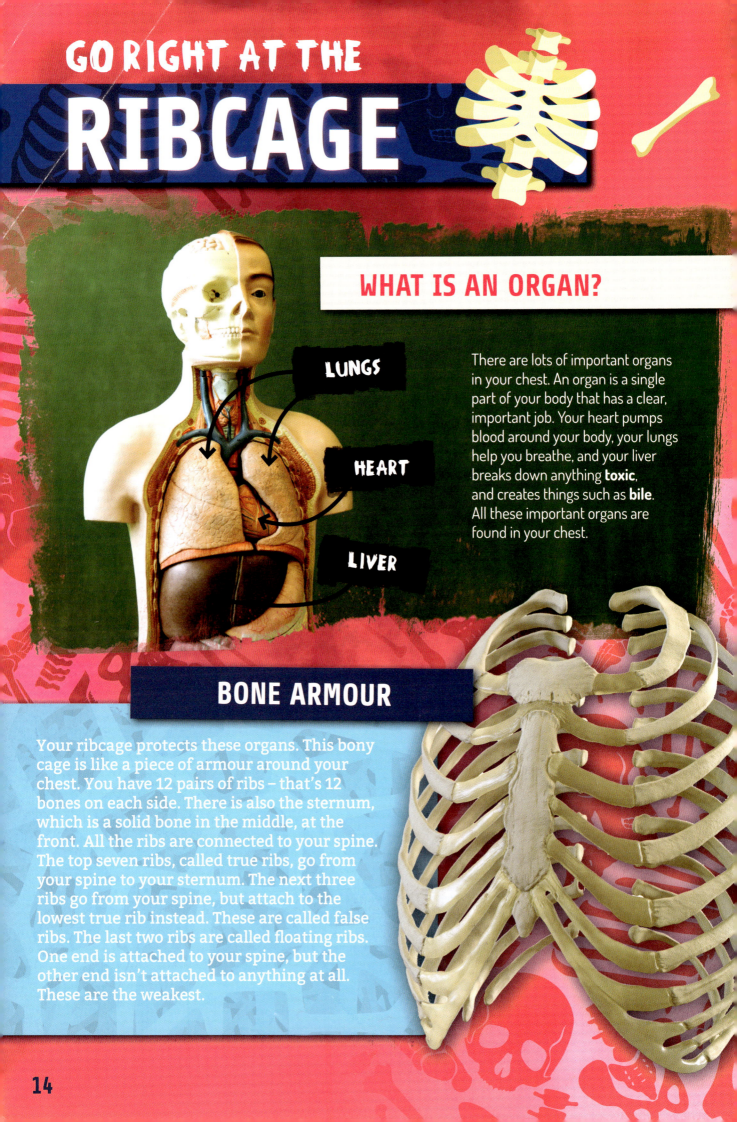

WHAT IS AN ORGAN?

LUNGS

HEART

LIVER

There are lots of important organs in your chest. An organ is a single part of your body that has a clear, important job. Your heart pumps blood around your body, your lungs help you breathe, and your liver breaks down anything **toxic**, and creates things such as **bile**. All these important organs are found in your chest.

BONE ARMOUR

Your ribcage protects these organs. This bony cage is like a piece of armour around your chest. You have 12 pairs of ribs – that's 12 bones on each side. There is also the sternum, which is a solid bone in the middle, at the front. All the ribs are connected to your spine. The top seven ribs, called true ribs, go from your spine to your sternum. The next three ribs go from your spine, but attach to the lowest true rib instead. These are called false ribs. The last two ribs are called floating ribs. One end is attached to your spine, but the other end isn't attached to anything at all. These are the weakest.

RISE OF THE RIBS

The ribcage is more **flexible** than you think. There are muscles between the ribs that help lift them up and down. This is important because your lungs get bigger and smaller as you breathe in and out. The ribs have to move with the lungs so they don't get in the way of your breathing.

THE RIBS ARE ATTACHED TO THE STERNUM WITH FLEXIBLE CARTILAGE. THIS IS WHY THEY CAN MOVE UP AND DOWN.

BROKEN RIBS

If someone is in a bad accident, some ribs can become cracked or broken. This can take around six weeks to be repaired. Sometimes it takes a lot to break a rib – however there have been some people who have broken a floating rib just by sneezing or coughing very hard. Don't worry, though, it is very rare to break a rib like this.

DOCTORS USE X-RAYS TO TAKE A PICTURE OF BONES BENEATH THE SKIN. THIS X-RAY IS SHOWING BROKEN RIBS.

You might be thinking: what kind of suit of armour has holes in it, and can be broken by coughing too hard? Me too! I'm amazed it does such a good job of protecting us.

AROUND THE
ARMS

Hmm, something's not right here. I think there is something in this arm bone! Stand back while I hammer it to pieces!

Oh... there's nothing unusual in here. My mistake. I guess I'll have to put this back together. In the meantime, let's have a look inside...

MORE ON MARROW

Bone marrow is much softer than the rest of the bone. There are two types of bone marrow: red and yellow. Yellow bone marrow is used to store fat. Fat is a type of nutrient that we get from some types of food. Fat is stored under the skin and inside bones, and the body uses it as backup **energy**. If the body can't get any energy from other types of nutrients, it will break down fat. We need a little bit of fat to stay healthy. However, if we have too much fatty food, we can become **overweight**. This is not so healthy.

BUTTER, FATTY MEAT AND CHOCOLATE ARE ALL EXAMPLES OF FATTY FOOD.

Red marrow stores cells which can become new blood cells. The marrow also helps break down old blood cells. When you are born, you only have red marrow in your bones. At seven years old, a lot of the red marrow begins to turn into yellow marrow. Adults only have red marrow in their skull, spine, hips, ribcage and at the end of the long bones in their arms and legs. However, the body can change yellow marrow into red marrow if it suddenly needs to create more blood.

BONE MARROW IS SPONGY AND FULL OF LOTS OF HOLES.

DIFFERENT TYPES OF BLOOD CELL

Red blood cells are pumped through veins around your body by your heart. They carry oxygen to different parts of the body. Oxygen is a very important **gas** that all parts of the body need to survive.

White blood cells fight illnesses and diseases. When harmful **bacteria** or viruses enter the human body, and make you feel ill, the white blood cells are sent out to destroy them.

HURRY OVER THE
HANDS

Where are we? Ah, wait, I know what bone this is! This is the distal phalange of the digitus minimus manus. You probably know it by another name – it's a pinky finger. We're in the hand!

THERE ARE 27 BONES IN THE HAND. THAT'S EVEN MORE THAN THE FEET.

WHEN JOINTS GO BAD

Bones can run into all sorts of problems. Aside from being broken, bruised or cracked, there can also be problems with the joints. This is a big problem for parts of the body like the hands and feet because there are many bones and many joints which can be affected.

PEOPLE WHO HAVE ARTHRITIS CAN GO TO A DOCTOR TO HELP THEM WITH THE PAIN.

ARTHRITIS

Arthritis is a **condition** where the cartilage in the joints is worn away. This usually affects older people. Arthritis can happen because the cartilage slowly wears away over time, or it can happen because white blood cells attack the cartilage around joints accidentally. Arthritis can cause joints to become stiff and painful as the bones rub together. Sometimes the bones can even be forced out of their proper place, or the joint can change shape. The joints might look bigger than normal.

HOW TO LOOK AFTER YOUR BONES

Some people's bones are stronger than others. There are lots of things you can do to make sure you grow up with healthy, strong bones. Eating a **balanced** diet will help your skeleton. Foods with lots of calcium are good for your bones. Here is a list of food and drink that will help you keep a super skeleton:

MILK

NUTS

BROCCOLI

BREAD

CABBAGE

TOFU

It is also important to get vitamin D. We get vitamin D from sunlight, so make sure you get outside every day. Food like eggs, fish and some breakfast cereals are also full of vitamin D.

KEEPING ACTIVE

Exercise is also important for building healthy bones. Sports such as football, basketball or tennis are a good way of getting exercise. Anything where you move around a lot, like dancing, running or playing on the playground are also good ways to exercise. This will make your bones super strong.

KEEPING YOUR BONES HEALTHY IS ESPECIALLY IMPORTANT AS A CHILD BECAUSE THIS IS WHEN BONES ARE GROWING.

SHARP LEFT AT THE
SHOULDER

This looks like the shoulder! Hmm, this one looks like it was broken in the past. Not by me, for once. It seems to have healed, though. You knew bones could heal, right?

HAVE YOU EVER BROKEN A BONE?

Breaking a bone can be very painful, especially if it is a big one in your arm or your leg. However, sometimes people hurt themselves but don't realise that they've broken a bone at all. This is more common with smaller bones, such as those in the hands or feet. However, most of the time it causes a lot of pain. People can also dislocate their bones. This means the bone slips out of its joint.

A BROKEN BONE CAN ALSO BE CALLED A FRACTURE, BUT IT MEANS THE SAME THING.

Someone who has broken a bone will probably have difficulty moving that part of the body. The area around the break might also swell up, or there might be a rough, grating feeling when the bone is moved, as if something is not right. The place where the bone is broken might look twisted or smaller too. Some people also feel sick or dizzy after breaking a bone.

THIS PERSON HAS BROKEN A FINGER.

HOW TO MAKE A BROKEN BONE BETTER

If you break a bone, you will have to go to the hospital. There are different **treatments** depending on which bone has been broken, and how badly. Usually the part of the body with the broken bone is put in a cast. A cast is a very strong type of bandage made of a type of material called plaster. The cast holds the bones in the right place while they heal. It can take weeks or months depending on which bone has been broken.

NOT ALL BONES CAN BE PUT IN A CAST. THERE IS NO WAY TO PUT A CAST AROUND THE RIBS, SO THEY ARE LEFT TO HEAL ON THEIR OWN.

CAST

HOW DOES A BONE HEAL?

A BONE HEALS ITSELF IN FOUR STEPS:

1 First, blood covers the break, then clots. This means it gets thicker and stickier.

2 A bridge of tissue is made between the two pieces of bone, called a callus. It is made of a type of cartilage.

3 The callus turns into a bone callus, which is like a hard shell that protects the break.

4 Then body slowly **replaces** the callus with harder bone tissue. The bone callus slowly fades away, and the bone looks normal again.

AT THE HOSPITAL, DOCTORS WILL GIVE PATIENTS MEDICINE TO TAKE THE PAIN AWAY AND LINE THE BONES UP IN A CAST. BUT APART FROM THAT, BONES HEAL ALL BY THEMSELVES.

NECK

Aaaaahhhhhhhh – OW! Oh no, I've hit his neck bone! I'm a silly Seymour! OK, if the patient complains about a pain in the neck when he wakes up, just tell him he must have slept on it funny. Luckily there are no breaks or bruises – his bones must be strong. I guess now is a good time to tell you about how bones grow to be like these ones...

X-RAY OF A BABY

GROWING

Babies and small children have different kinds of bones. Not only do bones get bigger as people grow up, but they also change a lot on the inside. Babies' bones are mostly made from cartilage, but that will change as they get older.

CARTILAGE

Cartilage is made from a lot of natural **fibres** that are stuck together in a gel-like tissue. It is softer than bone, but harder than muscle. This makes it perfect for certain parts of the body, such as joints, because these parts need materials that will bend.

As children grow up, the cartilage in their bones is slowly replaced with bone cells. The bone cells use calcium to do this. Not all the cartilage is replaced, but by the time someone is 30, their bones will be much harder and **denser**. This is because there is much more bone than cartilage. The bones stop becoming denser after the age of 30.

BABY

CHILD

ADULT

YOUR SKELETON SLOWLY REPAIRS AND REPLACES EVERY PART OF ITSELF OVER TIME. IT TAKES AROUND 10 YEARS FOR EVERY CELL TO BE REPLACED. THIS MEANS YOU HAVE A COMPLETELY NEW SKELETON EVERY 10 YEARS.

WHEN SOMEONE GETS TALLER QUICKLY, IT IS CALLED A GROWTH SPURT.

Bones get bigger, too. This is what makes a person taller. Bones keep getting bigger until someone is around 24. Bone grows fastest between the ages 11–18. These are usually the ages when teenagers get taller very quickly. A person won't get any taller after around 24, although they may get slightly smaller when they are a very old person. This is because the vertebrae in their spine get closer together.

TRAVEL PAST THE
TEETH

CROWN

THE ONLY BIT OF
THE SKELETON YOU CAN SEE

Your teeth are part of your skeleton too, although they do not count as bones. They are used to bite and chew your food, so that it is all mushed up by the time it reaches your stomach. The tooth is made up of two main parts: the crown and the root. The crown is the top part that you can see. The root is the bit that is stuck in your gum. It keeps your tooth in place, and also has nerves and blood vessels running through it.

ROOTS

TEETH ARE MADE UP OF THREE LAYERS:

1 The outside of the crown is covered with enamel. Enamel is the hardest thing in the human body.

2 Dentine is the middle layer. It is not as hard as enamel, and is a lot more like bone.

3 The inside layer is called the pulp. This is where the tiny blood vessels are which keep the dentine healthy.

Oh! Hello, my lovely assistant! I didn't expect to see you on this page so soon! No, of course I wasn't stealing this golden tooth, I was just, er... cleaning it! Yes... cleaning...

You will have two sets of teeth in your life. The first are called milk teeth, or baby teeth. They are different to your adult teeth – they are not as strong, and the roots are thinner. These thin roots are a different shape, which lets them fall out easily when your adult teeth are ready to grow. Baby teeth usually start to fall out after you are six years old.

IT DOESN'T USUALLY HURT WHEN MILK TEETH FALL OUT.

CHILDREN USUALLY HAVE A SET OF 20 MILK TEETH. ADULTS USUALLY HAVE A SET OF 32 ADULT TEETH.

THE FOUR TYPES OF TEETH

MOLARS are the strongest teeth, at the back of the mouth. They grind the food up into a mush, until it is ready to be swallowed.

INCISORS are at the very front of your mouth. There are four on top and four on the bottom. They are flat and thin, and are used for cutting and chopping, such as when you first bite an apple.

CANINE teeth are sharp and pointy, either side of your incisors. There are four of these in your mouth. They are used to tear tough food.

PREMOLARS are wider than incisors and canines. They are used to crush food into tiny pieces.

ENTER THE
EARS

You might be wondering what we are doing at the ears. Surely there can't be any bones in this floppy, wobbly thing? Well, it is true that the outside of your ear doesn't have any bones – it is made from cartilage. But what about inside the ear? Follow me down the ear hole to find out. I just hope that this guy has cleaned his ears recently...

BONES THAT HEAR

Deep in the ear are three very important bones. They are in an area called the middle ear. They are called the hammer, the anvil and the stirrup. They carry sound to another area called the inner ear. They also make that sound more powerful as it travels through the bones. This is important because the inner ear is full of fluid, whereas the middle ear is full or air. Have you ever tried to listen to sounds underwater? Most sounds become muffled and quiet. Only loud sounds can travel from air to water. Because of this, the ear bones need to make the sound more powerful to reach the fluid-covered inner ear.

WITHOUT THESE BONES, WE WOULD BARELY HEAR ANY SOUNDS AT ALL.

THE STIRRUP IS THE SMALLEST BONE IN THE BODY.

ANVIL

STIRRUP

HAMMER

1 Sound travels from the air outside and enters your ear. It **vibrates** the eardrum.

2 The eardrum is a piece of tissue which is stretched tight in your ear, like the skin over a drum. It is connected to the 'handle' of the hammer.

3 When the eardrum vibrates, the hammer moves too. The other end of the hammer is like a lever, and it moves the anvil.

4 The anvil is fused to the stirrup, so they move as one bone.

5 Finally, the stirrup is connected to something called the cochlea.

HAMMER

COCHLEA

STIRRUP

ANVIL

EARDRUM

THE COCHLEA LOOKS A BIT LIKE A SNAIL'S SHELL.

The cochlea is found in the inner ear, and its walls are made of bone. The cochlea takes the vibrations and then sends signals to the brain. The brain turns the signals into the sounds we hear. Different vibrations and signals will turn into different sounds in the brain.

27

STOP AT THE SKULL

BONE HEAD

The bones in your head make up your skull. There are two parts of the skull: the cranium and the facial bones. The cranium is the name of the bones that are around the brain, and they are there for protection. The facial bones give your face some of its shape. The jawbone is also one of the facial bones, and it is the only bone in your head that can move. This movement lets you eat and talk.

HUMAN SKULL

There are eight bones in the cranium. They are large and flat, and completely cover the brain. They are all fused together, and do not move at all. One of the bones at the bottom of the head, called the occipital bone, has a hole in it to let the spinal cord through. The spinal cord is connected to the brain. There are 14 bones in the rest of the skull.

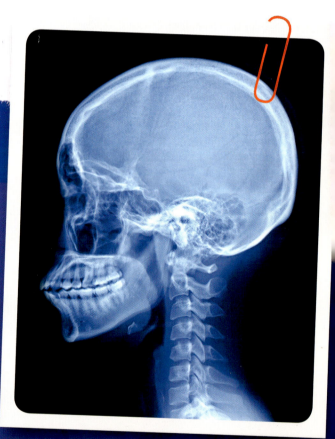

If I remember correctly, the skull is somewhere behind all this hard, white stuff. Huh, that's weird – we've reached the brain. Oh... oh dear...

THE ULTIMATE HELMET

Like the ribcage, the skull is mainly a piece of armour that protects something important. Unlike the ribcage, the skull has no holes, and is not flexible. That is because the brain is the most important organ, and needs extra protection. The skull is good at protecting the brain, although if someone receives a nasty bump to the head, they might get a concussion. A concussion is when the brain is knocked about inside the skull.

CONCUSSION CAN KNOCK SOMEONE OUT, GIVE THEM PAINFUL HEADACHES, OR MAKE THEM FEEL SICK OR CONFUSED.

SOFT AS A BABY'S... SKULL?!

When humans are born, the bones in the cranium are not fused together. This makes a baby's skull much softer than a child's or an adult's. In fact, there are even soft spots where the brain isn't fully protected. The biggest one is right on top of the baby's head. The reason the bones are not fused together is to make it easier when the baby is being born. After around 24 months, the bones in a baby's skull will fuse together, and the brain will be fully protected.

IT IS IMPORTANT TO BE VERY GENTLE WITH BABIES' HEADS AND AVOID TOUCHING THEIR SOFT SPOTS.

29

ALL
BETTER

Property of Seymour Skinless

Aha! Look up there, in the joint between those two bones! It's a medical clipboard. Er... some other tiny doctor must have left it here. This must be what is causing the patient so much pain. Let's grab it, and then get out of here.

Also, thank you so much for your help today. I couldn't have found this clipboard without you, my trusty assistant. Hopefully you learned a few things about the skeleton as well.

So now you know all about the skeleton. Isn't it incredible? Here are some extra bone facts.

HAVE YOU EVER HEARD OF THE FUNNY BONE? IT IS A PART OF YOUR ELBOW THAT CAN REALLY HURT IF YOU BUMP IT. IT IS NOT ACTUALLY A BONE; IT IS A NERVE.

THE ONLY BONE NOT CONNECTED TO ANY OTHER IS IN YOUR NECK, NEAR YOUR CHIN. IT IS CALLED THE HYOID BONE.

BONES ARE MADE UP OF 31% WATER.

GLOSSARY

ABSORB	to take in or soak up
AUTOMATICALLY	without conscious thought or control
BACTERIA	microscopic living things that can cause diseases
BALANCED	an equal amount of all things
BILE	a fluid that helps break down food
BILLIONS	one billion is one thousand million
BLOOD VESSELS	tubes in the body through which blood flows
CARTILAGE	flexible tissue found in joints and other places around the body, including the nose, ears and throat
CELLS	the basic units that make up all living things
CONDITION	an illness or other medical problem
DENSER	more tightly packed
ENERGY	the power required to make something work
FIBRES	thread-like structures
FLEXIBLE	easy to bend
FLUID	a substance that flows, especially a liquid
FUSE	to join and become one
GAS	an air-like substance that expands freely to fill any space available
GEL	a thick, jelly-like substance
LIMBS	the arms, legs or wings of an animal
NUTRIENTS	natural substances that plants and animals need to grow and stay healthy
OVERWEIGHT	(a person who) weighs an unhealthy amount
PRESSURE	a continuous physical force pushing on an object, which is caused by something pressing against it
REPLACES	puts back or in place of
ROTATE	turn around a central point
SIGNALS	signs or actions which give information or instructions
TISSUE	groups of cells that are similar to each other and do the same job
TOXIC	deadly or poisonous
TREATMENTS	medicines or using other ways to help cure a disease or heal an injury
VIBRATES	moves up and down, left and right or back and forth very fast
VIRUS	a microscopic thing which causes illness and disease in living things

INDEX